Virtualis

Topologies of the Unreal

David Dowker & Christine Stewart

BookThug · 2013

FIRST EDITION

The production of this book was made possible through the generous assistance of The Canada Council for The Arts and The Ontario Arts Council.

Canada Council for the Arts Conseil des Arts du Canada

ONTARIO ARTS COUNCIL CONSEIL DES ARTS DE L'ONTARIO
50 YEARS OF ONTARIO GOVERNMENT SUPPORT OF THE ARTS
50 ANS DE SOUTIEN DU GOUVERNEMENT DE L'ONTARIO AUX ARTS

LIBRARY AND ARCHIVES CANADA
CATALOGUING IN PUBLICATION

Dowker, David, 1955-
Virtualis : topologies of the unreal / David Dowker and Christine Stewart.

Poems.
Issued also in an electronic format.
ISBN 978-1-927040-62-1

I. Stewart, Christine, 1962- II. Title.

PS8607.098747V57 2013 C811'.6 C2013-901281-8

Printed in Canada

Virtualis

Contents

1. *Phantasmagoria, or the Empire of Senses*

No longer a phantasm and not yet a sign, the unreal object of melancholy introjection opens a space that is neither the hallucinated oneiric scene of the phantasms nor the indifferent world of natural objects. . . . The topology of the unreal that melancholy designs in its immobile dialectic is, at the same time, a topology of culture.

– Giorgio Agamben, *Stanzas: Word and Phantasm in Western Culture*

Patience arrays its strategies.[1] The blue sky faience
and the startling flows. Tincture of days passing.
Rapture of plant consciousness, suppliant plaintive
refrain. Sidereal inertia of the earth return posture
and the vibratory distances between dreams.

This time the vertigo is temporary. It effects a textuality
of sex. Brazen conjure. The medium is palladium
and hypostasizes. Its valence sighs
and lies upon the periodic table, maybe
radiant agency.

From the premonitory depths of the firing. A beam
of gauze hovers, pale northern glaze veils. The surface
of the lake of serene gleams.

Crystals, larvae, buds . . . *gemmules.*[2] Or
-ganiforms with felt hats and vivid fringes, fungus
tumuli. Reticulum of Her thought-fur murmurs.
(Something about this urn of a world.) Quivering
telepresence within the furniture. These retinals
and nerve-wing things fluttering about
the telling.

---

[1] "Patience details its follies."

[2] "I might have seen all that this single ray awakened of crystals, buds, and worms, in this beam." Arthur Rimbaud, "The Pool of Beth-Saïda."

the earth return posture

In the rapt inertia of this posture
I substitute the impunity of my civilizational
other[3] for your furniture and your teeth.
This secures me from the dread of selvages;
I mean of the human shape; I mean
of this urn world, where you are
my vivid fringe, my disordered subject;
where the moment of nation is
fission, and the ring of the massacre
is fashion for the last of the godly.

[3] "my civilizational other never flocked, never labelled the internal coherent"

this urn world

Here are the improbables and the multilated
whose (theoretical) spin is spindled with feral delight
as history does the hominid wobble. Language
dwells in the lulls, lingers lovingly in the lap
-ses, lazuli and gladioli my fetishes
so gland me your vocabulary
(or the book of your coterie).

I ignore those corrosives and the admonishment of
my (hypothetical) advisors for your inflorescence, for your
sheer fervour. Raw silk sheet (a flag or banner) torn from
our bed of salvages. After impassioned nations
arrive at the table, dishevelled and wild-eyed, simply
ravenous. Godness infiltrates at bright angles to
the representations of light.

gladioli my fetishes

My frenetic bent
was your ambivalence.
My spent intensity, your civic dissent.

And so I knit the fetish splint.
For phantasy is virtuality and I cannot resist
the insistence of its undulations,
its mirror site, its oval portal[4] – near
tar and error. Flung far

into the nether, the imaginations
are left to their own inverted devices
– apparent acceleration due to
time-dilation. Really
an eternity spent climbing the asymptotic
beanstalk . . . or shall we make a bee-line to
the blossoming? . . . (pre-) destination
over there.

---

[4] "My phobic truth was your discipline. My lush obscurity, your citizen lips. I prod this fetish twig for my fantasy is velocity and I cannot resist the liquid of its pronunciations, its oval site, its mirror."

the book of your coterie

I desire the robbery of my invention.

Your porcelain eternity splits the pleasure of my raze
and the golden sides from my propinquity.[5]

For example, I cannot wed the yellow deficiency in bloom.

For example, I devise the mimic – for fruitless took
my promising boy (oh odious despite gate)

for example,
and acceleration – the surface is fleshed out

for example,
a ripe detour (west) toward a citizen kiss

for example,
blossoms of aluminum

for example,
the line – etc., bean dark skull and succour

---

[5] Nips quick – a bug link.

out of whatever
abject idiolect

emergent verdant being

sibyl/line in kind
and taking a shine to
the slime trail

stratagems
glitter
in the murk furtive
alternity secured against
the vertebral multilingual
promise of this
vagrant kiss

bright angles

Gnosis bleed and speed burn . . . tastes like adrenaline
. . . surface glossed . . . ghost firing . . . temporal conduit.

I cannot weed the chaffed from the plumage.

I will devise compliance with fruitful respite
– o melodious gait. For example, praised
as above is, as below to grub in the rubbings
(and glow).

My naive conveyance dangling from the vine,
plum(b)ed with aplomb, be got(ten) mit(t)

foot / flesh / grass / neck.

Gloved vacuum and found a loophole. Line
drawn and re-drawn, darker than before
or sunder erasure.

gloved vacuum

This furtive law loops the finger of errant bliss.

It knits the dark.

No gnostic stock,
but a flesh plumb
& luck neck – a drawn object.

Naive vacuums suck the darkened bit.

(No prudence is mine palladium; no gauze, my succour.)

Their cult of love is the asylum of your wit.

Thus,
think gnaw.

Thus, think
creases
(impious)

in a vertebral light.

flesh plumb

The taste of theory in the back of the throat.
Bitter sediment, *seulement*. Golden seal upon
parchment lips. Tongue a quiver of slippages.
Glottal stop, not. Concave effacement.
Lattice
dowse
in the presence of such displacement.
Litmus viscera discipline. Sorrow is round
but emits sparks when squeezed.

Hybrid dynasties of carcinogenic saffron blossom
across the apocalyptic centuries. Carmine tines
of the migration into light –
another bloody mistake, mistook umbrage
with fruiting bodies in likely nightshade
and the hallucinatory lines of flight
of radicalized capital.

the taste of theory

at the back of this taste is paper
its bitter lattice
is not fruit but hallucinate

these lines cross douse
a glottal doze, a vessel ridge
or quiver is

read this lavish sobbing sense
throw this orange gaze
to the wick of your swallow

aside: we thought and it wrought –
as if it were weather or morning,
as if it were hollow
or forming

a glottal doze

verisimilitude
s h i m m e r

nested interests
implicit in

psyche knot entirely
apostrophized
(think lynx)
scientia cups
the quickening
d i s t r i b u t e d
being-thing

nested interests

tread this light-path lithely
lavish such leafy sundries upon
a drowsy multitude

given and the thickening
of the thought does not
tarnish hardly
stumbles once bitten

whether hallow or harrow
wile by witch-remote
antidotal shoulder to liaison upon
or aporia over

aver (a veer) further
read ochre
write reed head

Wind is auditory.[6]

Water is a matter of some urgency.[7]

This is the record of our reverberrations
in the soft impedance of time.

---

[6] It has no physiological feet or feed as convenient as its pure tones.

[7] My hubris, your rubbed hue of borage.

another bloody mistake

the striped heat flickers in peripheries
meaning to be inconspicuous but once spotted
cannot resist interpolation

the rotation of light through this
pliant medium mediates

the air *typically* insulates

chlorophyll is cunning and left to its own devices
suffices

embodiment is temporary
and serves

scarlet in the abstract
livid (or blush enough)

by another name[8] arose
incarnadine

and seen to be
leaved[9]

---

[8] Rosa Sélavy.

[9] Lounging in verdure, at languid angles of declination.

blush enough

the myth of Hir radiance
(inferred from the infrared)
in the form of articulate
heat enters as relation
(the world swallows its tongue)
streams curve, herding –
they impersonate a buoyant joy

it is uncut; it is previous
(being so reposed)
so arbitrary, therefore
no thrust, no lift; no stake, no fit

so the State sits in
for our civic frisk
and the Figural
functions as lack, illicit
dialectic[10] – the faciality
of my beloved
interlocutor, semiotic
eye contrived by luminosity –
terrestrial, signifying, despotic[11]

---

[10] It sucks – proptosis.

[11] "An effect of capturing a surface that becomes more enclosed the more it expands. This is the signifying despotic face and the multiplication proper to it, its proliferation, its redundancy of frequency." Gilles Deleuze and Félix Guattari, *A Thousand Plateaus.*

buoyant joy

they flaunt immensities,
utter brilliant dissonance,
dispense with most coherent
and high restraint abiding
consolation, in surges
furled, fondly surrounded,
nonplussed and be-plumed,
appalling heaps
of sleep at their feet,
the assumption of
the quotidian flinches,
startling things sing

being so reposed

It is in voluble struggle.

It forms a discourse, not a depiction.

Given to despair as a method of dance.

It is conduit and articulate drum.

Blot estimate tremor dwell seldom anticipates spate
(enthusiasms dissipate . . . pulsesetpitchinteger).

Gamut reel.

Pale and furious miracle of elucidation . . . gone spectral.

Block temporal. Slipped advent. The literal message is:
"It hasn't happened yet."

gone spectral

in the melancholia of the mirror is an egg and its aura

(another amour hammer – enamoured:
your tact to depict – goad domain foment)

scroll it back to
the ordered semi-sections
semi-dark (cathect words
like horde or horror)

a livid oil fetches a buckling mouth

I never saw again Aegean Ocean & him more likable, floating

(oh, wet rushy baby – just plucked up)

goad domain

overt burgeon, bevel upward and rude
toward light, loud lustre of apotheosis
in plain raiment refulgent

(my enamel is your dispatch & tent)

the veritable rubbing thrill
its rival
the lank and frugal

our wet nouns spell spill, spell
bitter peal to predicate these poly-plush buttons, fall
full to a floral imperative
asunder anew

the telling

It is incurable reinvention. These trees
mistaken for identity. She (Heredity)[12]
imitates water, weaves compliancies,
splices bliss. This cherished image
drawn in light lustrates, drowns
reticence. The glossy promise of
a wholly modal logos kiss
disinhibits. The ineluctable trajectory
of some sun-impelled arrow
overtakes me.

---

[12] Figura biologica.

Genus is dissolute. Vagrant is its range.[13] It is the logical effluvium
of some proto-binomial urge. Brute geogeny overwhelms
ontology. Basic array of itinerant fragrance and mute fruition.

Spaces are their own bloom. A gauge of any and several
congenital avowals. This rate brain interpretation
lichen aligned phosphorus chorus to appall us (o
rhodopsin bop voluptuary).

To divulge is lysergic (time-section light-thought in lilt).
It is febrile nostalgia. Rapt state. Atavistic splendour of
that chymical epoch.

There are silences, manias . . . convalescence.

Distractions avalanche here. See selah – a
shapely cadence. The converted word installed
in perfect retrograde.

[13] "Genus is difficult. Range is its sum."

Figural shells unravel in apparent (spectral) narrative
infiltration. Here secure channels lie fallow, hidden
in brightness or dark carnal hollows.

Our vocabularies maintain subjective principles
not immediately apparent as the (inexplicable)
lure of verdure.

chymical epoch

This is not a seance.[14] Escape is not an object.

The habit of synaptics matters yet still one fumes and stares
and wonders just what kind of trees are these.

We are gathering interior circumference.

Flecked bits, motes lit (dendritic).

Their truth is folded into bitter distance.

They face that solemn green arousal with oblique strategies[15]
of psychic detachment.

[14] "This is a science."

[15] For example: "Honour thy error as a hidden intention." Brian Eno and Peter Schmidt, *Oblique Strategies*

II. *Grid Meridian*

I find something – like language – immaterial, yet terrestrial, something circular that returns to itself across both poles while – cheerfully – even crossing the tropics: I find . . . a meridian.
– Paul Celan, *The Meridian*

It went out, and like a woman it was happy.

It was (primarily figural)
effaced in the limits in between
– where separation is
ratiocination, aligned
in fascination.[16]

It preceded the meat.[17]

It unfurled outward – continued
indexical (for example):
liminal imperative,
littoral differential,
the one
conundrum contango –

cerule, exiled.[18]

---

[16] Or anagrammatic (or saturnalian) INFO: a faint icon, a cat anon, & neaps.
[17] As figural as awning I am sheathed (and shorn); as a man I am Om (hi mom!) and mown.
[18] Rogue monogene.

indexical (for example)

Panegyric for all
intensive purposes, a virtuous immersion
in the dream lives of other object(ive)
(im)personalities, and then
some
sense of impending
declension. The disambiguation
of these velocities and the celestial mechanics
of a romanticized chromaticism,[19] slightly nervous
circuits secured against transubstantiation.[20]

---

[19] Ultralunar decoherence.

[20] Elemental disposition of forms means means of production are immaterial. If a tetrahedron could speak we would be tetrahedronal.

a romanticized chromaticism

The figure was elusive
and procedural – it was like a person.
It was happy in the allegory
and allusive in the naming
of separation.[21]

After all is said and
sadly forgotten. Only
commotion endures.
Figuratively speaking,
a literal reading would be
water under the bridge
or a door can be a jar.

[21] In colour sunder, in the tuned eras between ears, echo-locate, ignite.

a literal reading

It was happy . . . and it rained
on the effaced limits and the gentle coliseum
of its separation.

The sky opened to water
that fell mute and nude
upon the open incunabular arms
and cross-hatched mouth.
And we streamed before the commotion
before the naming, before the concupiscence
it was all distance and delirium, before
the subject and its summer.

And so we endured . . . and we wore its spectacle

and in the commotion
and the silence of the figure who ran like recognition
we watched the marathon of completion
in pre-natal repetition.

We had seen her before.[22]

---

[22] A retina op.

We have seen here before.
Who can say what continued?
Who can say the distance between
the figure and the recognition of the figure?
There was a snake and its commotion
. . . and it was summer.

It was more than a matter of
transference. It was becoming
the over-determined gnosis of
being there, a mostly ghostly trace
of honey in the air, a superfluity
of melancholy.

the one conundrum

The saying made it glow.
Who can dispute the impulse
to resolution? The affections
displayed played across and upon
the articulated surface of another
hinged contingency. Eminent sheen
of what is and what has never been
or, as likely as not, an
indeterminate species of heat
shimmer.

hinged contingency

It resonates – graphological
and ornate – indiscriminate
as our affections. At its gate
we hesitate. The florid
pen is poised. It inks
a curved hurl to
an indeterminate shoe.

Who can dispute the disgust
of the resolution? The tepid edits
of putti or a duped tit's riff. Twigged
upward to the curling peaks of green,
pent-up contention bleats.

a curved hurl

There's a hole in its soul
that the world passes through.

If only such unseemly decoherence
wouldn't be so insistently non-local.

The global default goes to
motive. That is that. Not that.
It matters.

unseemly decoherence

Call it locus or noon.
It still amounts to
a measure – a votive
manner.[23] Time's a pole
stunt – a commensurable
parable, an aural fissure
insistent with object
(auratic or fetish)
when in wherever
in aphasia I mean amnesia
where everything is
nothing. Or anything.

---

[23] Pieta rhetoria.

insistent with object

By all means let polar opposites repose,
transfixed contraries so disposed.
These flowers of delirium blossom
in that aporia, a frenzied catatonia
or raving calyx array, a mutant line
to a smooth space engendered,
the implicit lucidity of the body
in the near fields of the unreal.

for Rimbaud

Imagine the figure seeming.
Imagine the figure singing, coming.
Its face, a nascent egg.
Waning, wrinkled forgetting – sad, eh?

Ash transfixes it
in the fields of id[24]
– yellow corn pricks its angst,
the skin akin to ink.

From matter to baffle.
It is a slow takeover . . . incremental
exposure. The whole thing has a distinct odour,
humming. The sharp smell of summer's clearing,
coming: an orphic buttock, a swollen hue –
in tangible slabs of absence, fissures of absinthe.

And the finches bunch,
in its labial abutments, singing,
sighing as if nature were affable
or preternatural. And it's
eating – a genital nibble
for the cannibal bit. Her head's
the adorable detail, listening to
the sound of a snail.

[24] It is insurgent & outside precise eidetics.

A passionate impasse impinges upon the object of such attention
as madness and folly mop the floor with immobility.
This could be the beginning of

transference divergence. At the edge of a meadow a
-nother blasted path, a lapse proactive shatters. That
was the end of that. Now to the noumenoun.

The circular error is in the pudding.
A disproportionate portion of *****
pending redaction, the like thereof.

Aptonymic it
flatters, impresses (wax) –
as cogito ergo incants:
staccato & phatic,
to mimic, as manner,
the unspeakable portion
of the familiar,
ergo an impasse –
for matter lags (immaterial).

That is, as fax – we are not
known, but lapped up in phallus
(not phalanx: a sight unseen – some
ulterior bundle of stamens).

But now to the noumenon and pending:

the anus is an almond; the anus is a famous almond;
the anus is a famous almond cooling in that pudding.

Both could be amiably referred to
as reason enough to believe.
We might as well be illuminated
as actuarial, or a wavy maybe
apocalyptic dip. That is,
the fix is in.[25] The site of much
suchness is a far sight better than
merely near. Imagining
conspicuous absence. Here
it is.

[25] Concupiscence quotient noticeably holding firm.

a wavy maybe

Seen and unseen, an errant
strophe and catastrophe.
The eye is as apocalyptic as
reason (a hypnagogic plinth).[26]
Medusa whistles a medulla
obligata (cantata) – her
symptom's a riotous wave,
fluent in fixation wherefore
. . . sthenic then whence
sums come from, some
pressure on a nerve or
the ruins of this nevertheless
intermittent limit-field
in various similitudes
of swoon.

[26] The day is lipid, your toque baroque.

strophe and catastrophe

Haptic plank to be walked,
to wile a way to warble what
for and may be immutable,
smoothable curves merge
where mathematics fails
to amuse. One might imagine
wonder would be wider than
this. The occasion of this
artifice is the shared space
of suspended disbelief.

for Baudelaire

It loses the object
because the object is not
lost . . . It sleeps . . .
acedia (a deep snooze)
in the demon noon.

It curves to the in-folio of owls
gnarled on a damp tongue's rose[27]

. . . a baroque musick drifts down

. . . clutches its fleshy husk,
sings to the fervent cities – disperses
history in the non-neutrality
of a louche human
(the subject assumed).

Our melancholia is just
plush and uncivic.[28]

---

[27] Read ruse (or . . . finiculate).

[28] As Ophelia's arse – anise please!

fleshy husk

. . . and leaning over it watched the sound
and read the lines' brilliant lickt edge
– there, our oceans swelled, pelted
by the turbulent mouths that begged to be
fed their continual desires, rebooting
the generic slog of what was begot[29]

(to say that was involuntary would be inaccurate)

the way a hole shows green
the way music reminds me
the way this version beats to the hum of a ventilator

there, those stairs were as rigid as pleasure
as roped and fluted as skin, the radio was
as irreversible as a river
(as headlands are for cannibals)

chronus hovered over (us)[30]
in a whim blown indeterminacy

---

[29] alluvial splurge surfeit aberration contra-dicts, disses its/elf

[30] under recalcitrance since cinched this disconsolate junction sprung

whim blown

I is a tense in which
we are embodied
spurious distance baffles
the matter of its arrival
not a complete silence
but a depot woven[31]
not one single ele-
mental but
a genital unsettling
these extremes need
must accommodate
some transit interval
of all who ever
upon what sullen oath renascent
answered that irrational floor

[31] akin to diffusion, aligned to askewed ellip/tick demotic wird grid

some transit interval

ah ox, a hoax hole – it's slick by the river (out back a bit).
a wet rib, a shell's bend – arms out, furious wave – hey!

54 chronos eats these anecdotes (time and time again)[32]

omit stick – dim flicker far away
adjust a plain ankle stave – kith and clade allayed –
most post-ballistic . . . nirvana aquifer
inexplicably pentecaustic

[32] repeat re:mote at status that flagrant diagony angle struc(k)t

nirvana aquifer

symmetry of the trees
in spinal alignment[33]
these eyes to raise
an aberrant gaze
adjunct influx
through kindred conduits
vagrant root derivative
or lapsed gradient
to love's gambit advance
an oneiric recticulum
android radio aspires to
integral conditions
and vatic trajectories
amid auricular sumac

[33] centripetal and dorsal

lapsed gradient

. . . for whose extruded pleasure then
the starry pantomime, what lustrous beneficence
bestowed upon whose bent shoulders,
strife's damage pageant diffracted
through myriad meantimes?[34]

. . . quintessential finches forage along the fringes
of consciousness

[34] Tantamount to fracking the topology of some sleep-derived reality.

The body is plural,
a congeries
of metamorphoses
– its engine
is difference, its dermis
absurd – a hinged incidence
in a terminal display.

In the topology of its sleep-
induced inflorescence
a red vulvic ruckus
of mucous (mobius)
– a slime trail to
the underwrit ruse
of snail and skull (all
atypical lip(id)s encrypted)
. . . in a discrete laboratory
of forgiveness (Her forgiveness):
corpus mysticum melusine.[35]

[35] Salome is seen . . . with a saint's head on a silver plate.

III. *The Flowery Realm of the Barricades*

A life contains only virtual entities. It is composed of virtualities, events, singularities. What one calls virtual is not something lacking in reality.
– Gilles Deleuze, "Immanence: A Life . . ."

as with the discourse of leaves
or roses in the throes of

becoming sorrow

so for the infinitesimal dis-
placement of the far margin

the slightest twitch
or quiver
rings of springs
in jittery space

elucidate

the theriocephalous promise
of the world to come, implicit

in that other phantasmal dis-
pensation, positively

sinthomatic

theriocephalous promise

which brings us to the inadvertent curvature of the argument

as if to mitigate
untime
-ly sightings
due to a porous
chronosphere

(posit deft logic
circuits or bit emit-
ters perhaps)

the Sphinx sits,
disconsolate, in-
fernal riddle
withheld, in-
communicado

a porous chronosphere

a once utterance remnant
an almost when sequestered,

half-glimpsed becoming

not entirely simultaneous
or contemporaneous with

the unconsummated signification
of the thing itself,

notwithstanding the eventual
suspension of the continuum

hypothesis, the living road as is
given, open to interpolation,

otherwise lamentation,

a misapprehension at that
anecdotal table of discontent

anecdotal table

In the baroque house
the walls do not have ears
or mouths to map the lapses.

The word is a silent image
– its optics teach you to linger

in the swollen intervals
of divergent whorls
and vaguely surface-like
appurtenances – glad stasis
of the indeterminate.

Its portion is orphic
and business as usual to the Fates
(who have a spectacular subroutine
enhanced by a blue euphoria of ceilings).

a spectacular subroutine

By chance happened upon
an autobot (not to be confused with
one of the bit-motes of the anthropo-genie)
in the process of disassembling the semblance
of an open space.

Dense,
hyper-tense
and insistent,
a micro-dot
among the phenomena,
it folds and unfolds itself,
programmed for auto-subjectivity,
disinhibiting in its disguises,
netherwise entangled.

Delirium exteriorized . . . the human diagram transmogrified
. . . prosthetic coupling through the intersoul . . . superimposed
surfaces within the furrows and folds . . . shades of scientia
sexualis.

the human diagram

Call this the introduction of the ellipses

. . . clamour under inscription

a strictly pictorial
rhythm . . . the thought-pop thing
of otherness itself . . . has no essence

no thing
but this nothing

. . . (body)
suspended above
a simultaneity

of gravity . . . of bees
and light

. . . h(e)ad . . . severed

apoplectic object

halo aura eye

delineate
organ of totality

a simultaneity

Behold the inglorious worm:
apostate programmatic problematic
evangel of the digital.
Hail not but beware
the advent of
the unravelling
of its multifarious arithmetic
from dark pools of
illicit liquidity,
hidden in
the interworld,
the very incunabulum
of rising forth
from the foam of
the moment
(to the criticality
of scopic regimes),
behold the amor-
phous chorus of
the irredeemably
mediated

Everything is gilded and giddy. Things stream, seemingly self-possessed and effortlessly cybernetic networks coalesce and vaporize, fissure and fold in voluminous blue. Geometric shapes loop – optical automata – gauze petals cross, graze, guzzle under pock-marked skies, purpled clouds spiralling up inner arms, turning above marbled domes, bobbing for nipples as dazzling as birds, as plumed as brides, as rhetorical as the real (congenital).[36]

In this abstracted state we felt the need to forget.

Ciborium simulates staves. Procession niche colossal relics borne in buoyant scrolls graze in flank's relief.

We were historic in our present (anamorphic). We imagined effects along mutually perpendicular lines, along folds of big contemplative screens.

---

[36] Return to the same object. Absorb its hysteria.

gilded and giddy

what else but the meanders
thus sustains us, as such
bumping into things, bristling
with the implacable mastery of
the disastrous consequence,
what no mere demarcation connotes,
a scrim residuum with a spot of motley
and a tip of the hat to that
experiential conflux,
besotted with the spectacle itself
– those adorable details, such as
the absence of mandibles or
the exaggerated gestures of
the psychically agitated –
a semblance engendered by breath,
immaculate anachronism to be
apprehended then
a superabundance of fullfillingness overflowing

blueblueblueblueblueblue*(impious)*bluebluebleubluebleublue
bluebluebluebluebleublue*(impious)*bluebluebleubleublueblue

A new tubule swerves to the smooth hue of crystallized mucous, a collated tryst (twick deep as nations mewl). An umber comma spreads its arms, fluid and rapid, as skyward as spun (collect, sort and frame). Its twinned legs reap (by the common authority of dreams).

Splayed shards we parse and call it memory. I is its hatchling – broken and bleeding from, I inculpates inchoate, hemorrhaging backwards as augered as the rose excised.

Under clotted skies a figure (rectilinear) in a loose weave speaks – *entrebescar*: she bathes.[37]

---

[37] Figura aporia.

para-sited by the light
(phantasmic), as through
dissolution that brightness
confound, concomitant occupation
by other emissaries of the Imaginary
and various semi-real entities,[38]
assorted sorties with centaurs
and centauresses, satyrs
and satyresses
(exemplary radioscopy)[39]
in alterity even
as in the continuum
a procession of essences and eminence
(so many oscillations across the ectoplasmic reticulum)

---

[38] "Substance being a real physical entity, – perceptions real physical entities, – matter, form, quantity, and so on, so many fictitious entities, both descriptions being in part applicable to space, neither of them applicable entirely, – space may be regarded and spoken of as a *semi-real entity*." Jeremy Bentham, "A Fragment on Ontology."

[39] "The baroque is the regulating of the soul by corporal radioscopy." Jacques Lacan, *The Seminar of Jacques Lacan, Book XX.*

that brightness confound

a breach (amphibrach):[40]

semantic waves flood
fields of glittering syntax,

luminous aggregates irradiate

"foreign" vernaculars

that snake thread-like into
branched sentences, baled

in the ruddy duality of capital
empaled in rhetoric of race,

order-words catch in the throat
of a spent leit-motif,

dissident neural clusters
sculpted in relief,

in this black amassing of leaves
I repeat my brief

[40] We plied the corporeal, plowed the literal.

a breach (amphibrach)

object ache[41]

each abject

stratification
collapses in
the culmination
which brings us to
the apex of
the inverse aversion,
spiritualized app-
liances hap-
hazardly rap-
tured, tri-
geminal peripherals
vibrate or gesticulate,
a squip quinty or
cryogene plasmate,
cryptic inarticulate
acetate say golgi
embodiment raised
inchoate waferthin
instrumentality

be that as it may

---

[41] The object is allegorical under the gaze of the melancholic.

I

Exemplum

The morning adorns their giddiness.

Tableaux

Her glory sits at an inexhaustible table.

He may (I foment) hear the foam of waves burst unto the fields.

II

Exemplum

Only the actors know and even they are astonished.

Tableaux

Among carved pillars a woman strolls, in the manner of an ambulatory puppet, past caparisoned elephants, camels, alligators, monkeys and marsh birds.

We are entwined in a serenity of vases; we are commingled with wine.

The portals are flooded, and full of petals.[42]

---

[42] Antinomies absent in abysmal bliss.

III

Exemplum

I wish to be saved but these fluctuating thoughts do not permit it.

Tableaux

Melancholy sits in the particulate, perceivable air. Her hand parts the air. Her cheek rests in air. Her mouth is air. She is for the most part the silent air.

It is cold and caterpillars stiffen. Fruit globes glisten in swollen bowls of granular light. Ants anticipate apocalypse, roll in twos, lug eggs and twist thoraxes, snug between time's drupelets.

IV

Exemplum

Till Oblivion flings them!

Tableaux

Something is happening . . . like beatitude, it expresses unequal tangled forms, broken objects, a kind of liminal tremor.

Nearly monochromatic, it waits: auratic, radiant and bleeding.

Seeing, touching, cutting, eating.

She is listening to a snail eating a flower.

Through agate to
a leafy whispering[43]
(a rustling of latencies)
wondering what in the world
happened to that other firmament,
not entirely sure there ever was another
or what could possibly be the reason for this
transition, being in the habit of climbing trees
to aestivate (o torpor o bliss) and not really
ideally situated to navigate the exigencies,
a somewhat redundant incumbency
seems to settle into this incarnation,
some psychogeographic emulsion
extended in a gesture of compassion
or the epitome of opacity, perhaps
lapsed ambivalence, enlightenment
understood to be inadvertent.

---

[43] "So a leafy whisper said." Thomas Lovell Beddoes, *The Flowery Alchymist.*

Some Readings

The Coming Community, Giorgio Agamben
The Open: Man and Animal, Giorgio Agamben
Stanzas: Word and Phantasm in Western Culture, Giorgio Agamben
Les Fleurs du Mal, Charles Baudelaire
"Paris, Capital of the 19th Century," Walter Benjamin
The Origin of German Tragic Drama, Walter Benjamin
"A Fragment on Ontology," Jeremy Bentham
Baroque Reason: The Aesthetics of Modernity, Christine Buci-Glucksmann
The Anatomy of Melancholy, Robert Burton
Tiepolo Pink, Roberto Calasso
"The Meridian," Paul Celan
The Fold: Leibniz and the Baroque, Gilles Deleuze
A Thousand Plateaus, Gilles Deleuze and Félix Guattari
Notes on Conceptualisms, Vanessa Place / Robert Fitterman
The Seminar of Jacques Lacan, Book XX, Jacques Lacan
Parables For the Virtual: Movement, Affect, Sensation, Brian Massumi
"Sensation," Arthur Rimbaud
Illuminations, Arthur Rimbaud

Acknowledgements

An early version of the first section of this book appeared in *The Alterran Poetry Assemblage.*

Translators of works quoted: *Stanzas: Word and Phantasm in Western Culture,* Giorgio Agamben, translated by Ronald L. Martinez; "The Pool of Beth-Saïda, Arthur Rimbaud, translated by Louise Varèse; *A Thousand Plateaus,* Gilles Deleuze and Félix Guattari, translated by Brian Massumi; *The Meridian,* Paul Celan, translated by Pierre Joris; excerpt from "Immanence: A Life . . ." by Gilles Deleuze in *Potentialities: Collected Essays in Philosophy,* Giorgio Agamben, translated by Daniel Heller-Roazen; *The Seminar of Jacques Lacan, Book XX,* Jacques Lacan, translated by Bruce Fink.

Christine would like to thank David Dowker, Ted Byrne and Salome.

About the Authors

DAVID DOWKER was born in Kingston, Ontario but has lived most of his life in Toronto. He was the editor of *The Alterran Poetry Assemblage*, and his first book, *Machine Language*, was published in 2010.

CHRISTINE STEWART lives on the North Saskatchewan River. She works at the University of Alberta and the Learning Centre in downtown Edmonton. Publications include *from Taxonomy, Pessoa's July: or the months of astonishments* and *The Trees of Periphery. The Humanist* is forthcoming from Red Nettle Press.

Colophon

Manufactured as the first edition of *Virtualis: Topologies of the Unreal* in the Spring of 2013 by BookThug.

Distributed in Canada by the Literary Press Group: www.lpg.ca.

Distributed in the United States by Small Press Distribution: www.spdbooks.org.

Shop on-line at www.bookthug.ca

BOOK
PRODUCTION
WAR ECONOMY
STANDARD

Type + design by Jay MillAr

Cover image: detail from "Allegory of Divine Providence and Barberini Power" by Pietro da Cortona